Caracals

Victoria Blakemore

For Maggie, my little caracal

Table of Contents

What Are Caracals?

Caracals are mammals. They are members of the small cat family. They are related to the serval and the African golden cat.

The caracal is sometimes called the African lynx, desert lynx, or the Persian lynx. However, they are not actually lynxes.

Caracals are usually dark red, gray, tan, and white in color. They are known for their black ears.

Size

Although they are members of the small cats, they are quite large. They can grow to be over three feet long and stand eighteen inches tall.

When fully grown, they usually weigh between fifteen and forty pounds.

Male caracals are usually

larger than female caracals.

Caracals have long **tufts** of black hair on their ears. They also have over twenty muscles in their ears. This allows them to move their ears in different directions.

They have long legs and a slim body, which helps them to run very fast.

6

Like other cats, caracals have
long whiskers. They help
caracals to sense objects
around them.

7

Habitat

Caracals are able to **adapt** to living in many habitats. They can be found in savannas, scrublands, woodlands, mountains, and **semi-deserts**.

It is usually very warm and dry where caracals live. There are lots of plants where they can hide to surprise prey.

Range

Caracals are found on the continents of Africa and Asia.

They are often found in India, Nigeria, Turkey, Iran, Egypt, and Zimbabwe.

Diet

Caracals are **carnivores**. They eat only meat.

Their diet is mainly made up of hares, mice, and antelope. They have also been known to eat ostriches and smaller birds.

Caracals have a very good sense of hearing. They use it to find their prey.

Grooming

Like many other kinds of cats, caracals **groom** themselves. They lick their fur to wash it and keep it clean.

Keeping their fur clean can make it easier for them to sneak up on prey. They are harder for prey to smell when they are clean.

Communication

Caracals use sound, scent, and movement to communicate with each other. Different ear movements are used to send messages to other caracals.

Caracals have a special scent that they use to mark their **territory**. It tells other caracals that the area is taken.

Caracals use sounds like

hisses, mews, growls, and purrs

to communicate.

Movement

Caracals are very **agile** animals. They are able to move and turn very quickly. They can run up to fifty miles per hour when chasing prey.

They are also able to jump very high. They can jump up to ten feet high, which allows them to catch birds in the air.

Caracals are very good at climbing. Their sharp claws and strong legs allow them to climb tall trees.

Caracal Kittens

Caracals usually have a **litter** of two or three babies. Their babies are called kittens. When they are first born, their eyes are shut. They open after about ten days.

Mothers stay with their kittens in dens. Their dens are usually old burrows from other animals.

Kittens stay with their mother for about one year. She teaches them how to hunt and survive.

Caracal Life

Caracals are usually **solitary**.

They spend their time alone.

Mothers and their kittens are

the only ones who spend a lot

of time together.

They can be very **aggressive**

when defending their **territory**.

They do not like other caracals

to get too close.

Caracals are usually **nocturnal.**

They are most active at night.

They often sleep and rest

during the day.

Caracals as Pets

In some places, it is **legal** to own a caracal as a pet. Their behavior can be similar to a pet cat.

Caracals can eat up to three pounds of meat each day, which can be expensive. They are also more likely to be destructive when playing.

Although caracals are a kind of cat, they are wild animals. They are not the right pets for everyone.

Population

Caracals are not currently **endangered**. There are many left in the wild. However, in some places, their populations are **declining**.

It is not known how many are in the wild. Caracals can be hard to find, so it is hard to know how many there are.

In the wild, caracals often live between twelve and fifteen years.

Caracals in Danger

Although caracals are not **endangered**, they are facing threats. Their habitats are being destroyed for roads, farms, and buildings.

In some places, caracals are killed by farmers. The farmers are trying to protect their **livestock**.

Caracals are often killed when trying to cross streets that run through their habitats.

Helping Caracals

In many countries, special protected areas have been set up. They provide animals such as caracals with a safe habitat to live in.

In some places, caracals are a protected species. They are not allowed to be hunted by people.

In countries such as India, researchers are studying caracal populations. They want to learn more about them so they can help them.

Some groups are working with farmers in places where caracals live. They want to reduce the **conflict** between people and caracals.

Glossary

Adapt: to change or adjust

Aggressive: mean, ready to fight

Agile: moving quickly and gracefully

Carnivore: an animal that eats only

meat

Conflict: fight or disagreement

Declining: getting smaller

Endangered: at risk of becoming

extinct

Groom: to make clean and neat

Legal: allowed by law

Litter: a group of animals born at the same time

Livestock: animals such as cows and sheep that are kept by humans

Nocturnal: animals that are active at night

Semi-desert: an area that is similar to a desert, but with more rain

Solitary: living alone

Territory: an area of land that an animal claims as its own

Tufts: a clump of strands of hair or fur

About the Author

Victoria Blakemore is a first grade

teacher in Southwest Florida with a

passion for reading.

You can visit her at

www.elementaryexplorers.com

Also in This Series

Gray Wolves	Sloths	Flamingos	Camels	Koalas	Honey Bees	Pandas
Pangolins	White-Tailed Deer	Orcas	Giraffes	Corn	Meerkats	Echidnas
Walruses	Raccoons	Bald Eagles	Apples	Arctic Foxes	Red Pandas	Cassowaries
Tigers	Ladybugs	Moose	Beluga Whales	Leopards	Elephants	Jellyfish
Dugongs	Lions	Dolphins	Reindeer	Hammerhead Sharks	Hippos	Pumpkins
Peafowl	Chameleons	Florida Panthers	Aye-Ayes	Black Bears	Cheetahs	Manatees
Gingerbread	Polar Bears	Hot Chocolate	Orangutans	Coyotes	Marshmallows	Strawberries

Elementary Explorers

Victoria Blakemore

Also in This Series

Elementary Explorers — Aardvarks — Victoria Blakemore

Elementary Explorers — Mako Sharks — Victoria Blakemore

Elementary Explorers — Alligators — Victoria Blakemore

Elementary Explorers — Frogs — Victoria Blakemore

Elementary Explorers — Hedgehogs — Victoria Blakemore

Elementary Explorers — Brown Bears — Victoria Blakemore

Elementary Explorers — Bongo — Victoria Blakemore

Elementary Explorers — Sea Turtles — Victoria Blakemore

Elementary Explorers — Quokkas — Victoria Blakemore

Elementary Explorers — Muskrats — Victoria Blakemore

Elementary Explorers — Zebras — Victoria Blakemore

Elementary Explorers — Red Foxes — Victoria Blakemore

Elementary Explorers — Ring-Tailed Lemurs — Victoria Blakemore

Elementary Explorers — Platypus — Victoria Blakemore

Elementary Explorers — Anteaters — Victoria Blakemore

Elementary Explorers — Kangaroos — Victoria Blakemore

Elementary Explorers — Rhinos — Victoria Blakemore

Elementary Explorers — Jaguars — Victoria Blakemore

Elementary Explorers — Wombats — Victoria Blakemore

Elementary Explorers — Capybaras — Victoria Blakemore

Elementary Explorers — Gorilla — Victoria Blakemore

Elementary Explorers — Cats — Victoria Blakemore

Elementary Explorers — Skunks — Victoria Blakemore

Elementary Explorers — Butterflies — Victoria Blakemore

Elementary Explorers — Dingoes — Victoria Blakemore

Elementary Explorers — Snow Leopards — Victoria Blakemore

Elementary Explorers — African Wild Dogs — Victoria Blakemore

Elementary Explorers — Penguin — Victoria Blakemore

Elementary Explorers — Whale Sharks — Victoria Blakemore

Elementary Explorers — Wolverines — Victoria Blakemore

Elementary Explorers — Warthogs — Victoria Blakemore

Elementary Explorers — Caracals — Victoria Blakemore

Elementary Explorers — Badgers — Victoria Blakemore

Elementary Explorers — Seals — Victoria Blakemore

Elementary Explorers — Humming — Victoria Blakemore

Elementary Explorers — Pikas — Victoria Blakemore

Elementary Explorers — Humpback Whales — Victoria Blakemore

Elementary Explorers — Pumas — Victoria Blakemore

Elementary Explorers — Lemonade — Victoria Blakemore

Elementary Explorers — Llamas — Victoria Blakemore

Elementary Explorers — Tulips — Victoria Blakemore

Elementary Explorers — Ostrich — Victoria Blakemore

Elementary Explorers — Sunflowers — Victoria Blakemore

Elementary Explorers — Fennec Foxes — Victoria Blakemore

Elementary Explorers — Sea Lions — Victoria Blakemore

Elementary Explorers — Squirrels — Victoria Blakemore

Elementary Explorers — Roses — Victoria Blakemore

Elementary Explorers — Porcupines — Victoria Blakemore

Elementary Explorers — Ice Cream — Victoria Blakemore